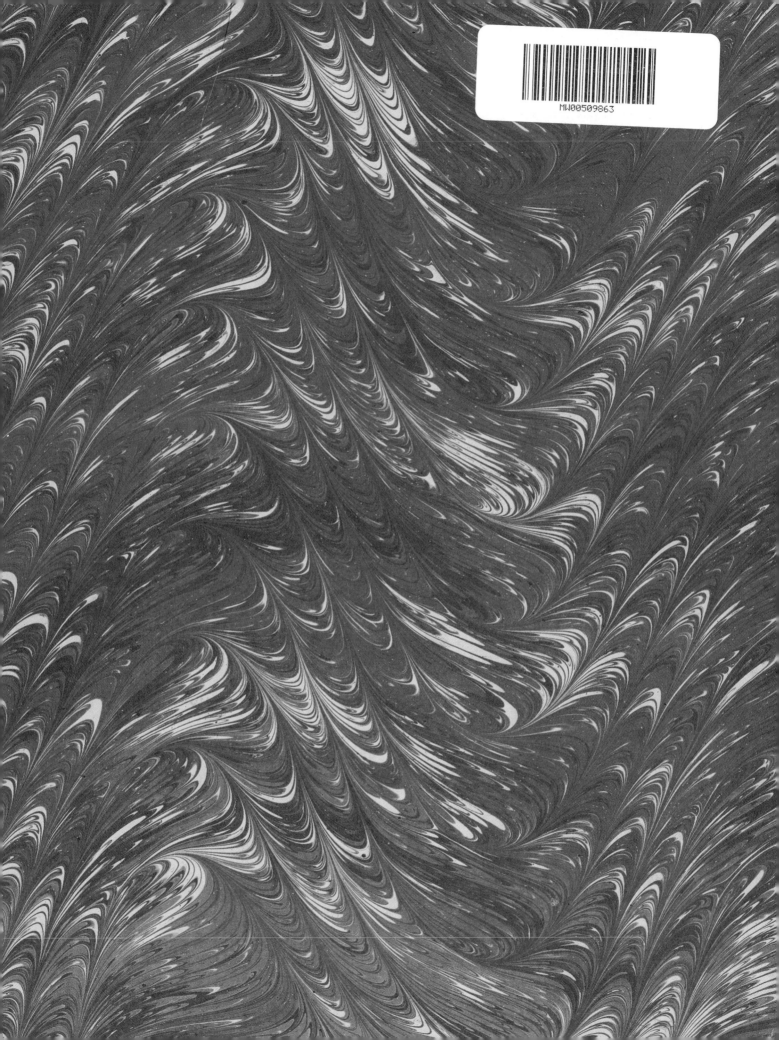

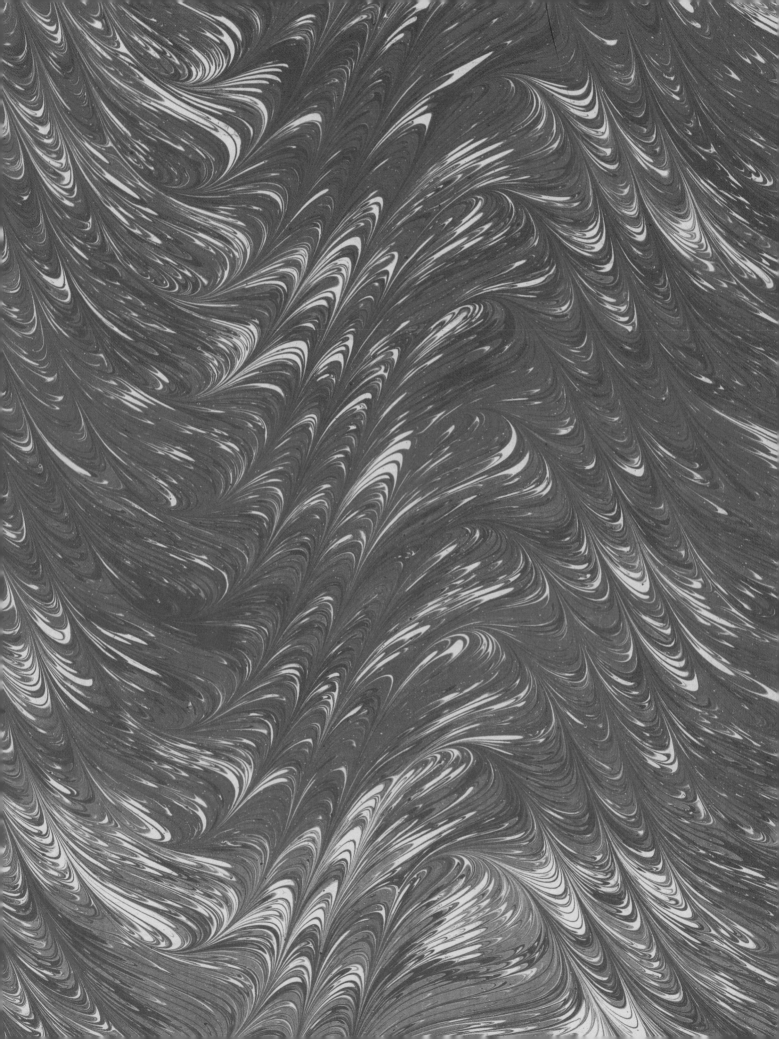

HARCOURT

· TROPHIES ·

A HARCOURT READING/LANGUAGE ARTS PROGRAM

HERE AND THERE

SENIOR AUTHORS
Isabel L. Beck ◆ Roger C. Farr ◆ Dorothy S. Strickland

AUTHORS
Alma Flor Ada ◆ Marcia Brechtel ◆ Margaret McKeown
Nancy Roser ◆ Hallie Kay Yopp

SENIOR CONSULTANT
Asa G. Hilliard III

CONSULTANTS
F. Isabel Campoy ◆ David A. Monti

Orlando   Boston   Dallas   Chicago   San Diego

Visit *The Learning Site!*

www.harcourtschool.com

Requests for permission to make copies of any part of the work should be addressed to School Permissions and Copyrights, Harcourt, Inc., 6277 Sea Harbor Drive, Orlando, Florida 32887-6777. Fax: 407-345-2418.

HARCOURT and the Harcourt Logo are trademarks of Harcourt, Inc., registered in the United States of America and/or other jurisdictions.

Acknowledgments appear in the back of the book.

Printed in the United States of America

ISBN 0-15-335586-7

3 4 5 6 7 8 9 10 048 10 09 08 07 06 05 04 03

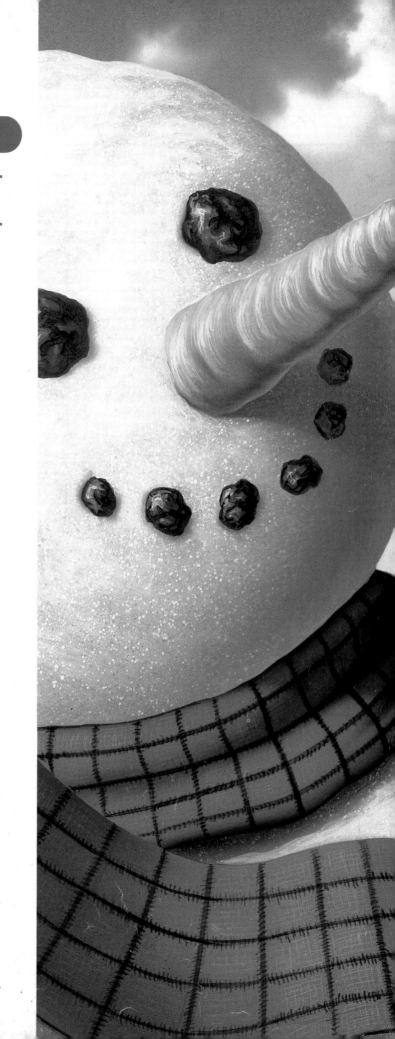

HARCOURT

· TROPHIES ·

A HARCOURT READING/LANGUAGE ARTS PROGRAM

HERE AND THERE

Dear Reader,

Welcome to **Here and There!** Adventures in books can take you to some amazing places. The adventures in this book take you to the world of butterflies, on a chase for a runaway dog, and to meet children just like you who love to play and work together. We hope you like these stories as much as we do!

Sincerely,

The Authors

The Authors

I Think I Can!

CONTENTS

Theme Big Books

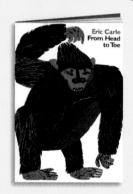

Decodable Books 13-18

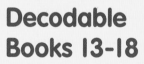

5

I Think I Can!

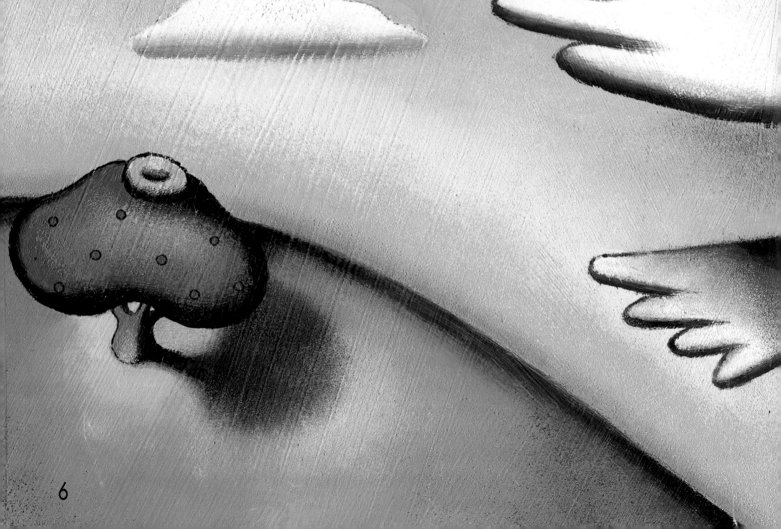

Word Power

Words to Remember

air

animals

around

fly

live

soon

turns

Many **animals live around** here. We **live** here, too. We **fly** in the **air** all day.

Soon the day will end. We look for a spot to stop. When day **turns** to night, we rest.

9

Genre

Nonfiction

Nonfiction books tell about things that are true.

Look for:

- Photographs that support what you read.

- Information that is given clearly.

I Am a

Butterfly

by Stephen Swinburne

Can you see me
on the plant?

12

I'm a little butterfly egg.
It's time for me to hatch.

Now I'm a caterpillar!

Wind fills the air. I hang onto a plant so I don't fall.

Lots of **animals** **live** **around** here.
I see a bug and a frog.

Lots of animal homes are here, too. I see a nest and a web.

Rain falls. It plips and plops.
I drink the small drops.

This plant is my food. I need
food so I can grow.

19

I eat and eat. I can't stop.
Chomp! Chomp!

20

I look for a spot to rest.
Soon I will shed my skin.

At last I am a chrysalis.
I'm an inch long.

In ten days, my chrysalis **turns** black. Then my snug home cracks, and out I come!

Look at me now!
I am an insect.
I have six legs.

24

My wings help me fly.

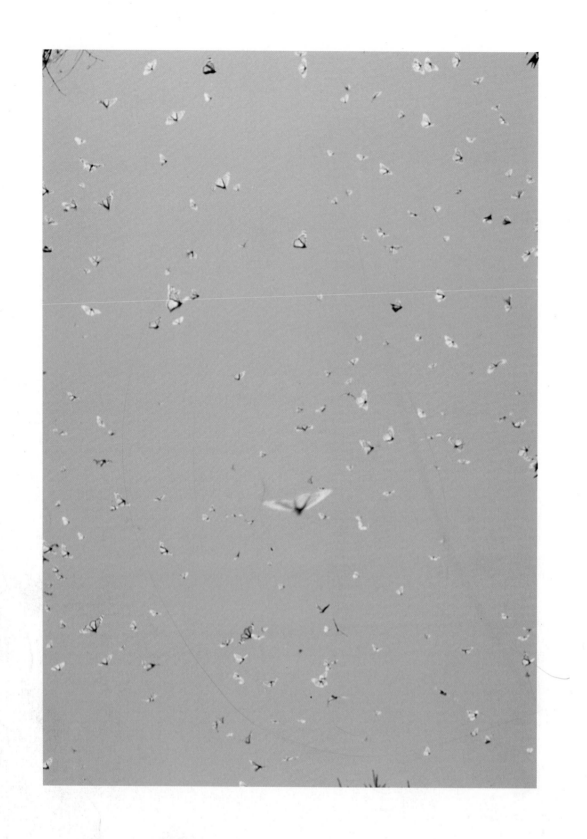

I like to fly with all my friends.

I am a butterfly!
I am a beautiful butterfly!

Think and Respond

1. What are the stages of a butterfly's life?

2. Why do you think the author has the butterfly tell its own story?

3. Why does the caterpillar eat so much?

4. What happens to the chrysalis?

5. Would you like to be a butterfly for a day? Why or why not?

Meet the Author/Photographer

Stephen Swinburne

Stephen Swinburne loves butterflies! He planted a big garden of flowers at his house to attract butterflies. He took the pictures for "I Am a Butterfly" in his garden. He hopes you have fun watching butterflies!

Mari Rosa and

by Charlotte Pomerantz

illustrated by Amy Bates

Mariposa, butterfly,
Mariposa, fluttering by,
Why oh why oh why can't I
Be Mariposa?

the Butterfly

Mari Rosa, dancing by,
Dancing, prancing, braids tossed high.
Why oh why oh why can't I
Be Mari Rosa?

31

Making Connections

More Insects

Like all insects, a butterfly has six legs. Find out about an insect. Draw it and tell something about it.

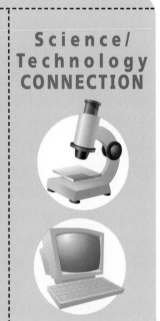

Butterflies have nice colors.

Good Eating

A caterpillar eats plants to grow. Plants give us healthful foods, too. List some foods you like that come from plants.

A Butterfly Poem

Create your own poem. Fill in the blanks. Draw a picture. Share your work.

Fly, butterfly!

Fly to ___.

See the ___.

Then fly home.

33

Words with <u>ch</u> and <u>tch</u>

The letters <u>ch</u> can stand for the /ch/ sound at the beginning of <u>chick</u>. What is another word that starts with the /ch/ sound for <u>ch</u>?

The letters <u>tch</u> stand for the /ch/ sound at the end of <u>watch</u>. What is another word that ends with the /ch/ sound for <u>tch</u>?

Name these pictures. Which picture does not have the /ch/ sound for <u>ch</u> or <u>tch</u>?

Read these words from "I Am a Butterfly." Where do you hear the /ch/ sound for <u>ch</u> and <u>tch</u>?

hatch   chomp   inch

Test Prep
Words with <u>ch</u> and <u>tch</u>

1. Which picture name has the beginning sound for <u>ch</u>?

  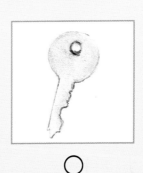

○   ○   ○

2. Which picture name has the ending sound for <u>tch</u>?

 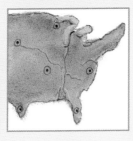 

○   ○   ○

Tip

Say each picture name very slowly. Listen to all the sounds before you choose an answer.

Word Power

Words to Remember

city

house

sometimes

take

there

Kim and Dad are new in the **city**. **Sometimes** they miss their **house** on the farm.

"Let's **take** a walk in the park," said Dad. "I'll bet our friend Mr. Sanchez will be **there**."

37

Did You

by Wong Herbert Yee

illustrated by Laura Ovresat

See Chip?

Kim

Dad

Chip

Mr. Sanchez

Hot Dog Man

Park Worker

 I miss our farm. I wish I had friends here in the city.

 Sometimes it's hard to be in a new house.

41

 Let's take Chip for a walk.
That will help us cheer up.

 Yip-yip! Yip-yip!

 Stop, Chip! Come back!

 We need to catch him! He
could get lost in this big city.
Let's go!

 Hi! Did you see my dog, Chip?

 Is he the little black dog with the yip-yip bark?

 That's our Chip!

44

I think he ran to the park.
I'll help you catch him!
Let's go ask the man at
the hot dog cart.

45

Hi! Did you see my dog, Chip?

Is he the little black dog with the yip-yip bark?

That's our Chip!

46

I think he ran to the swings. I'll help you catch him!

47

 Hi! Did you see my dog, Chip?

 Is he the little black dog with the yip-yip bark?

 That's our Chip!

48

I think he ran out of the park.
I'll help you catch him!

49

Look, there on the steps!
Isn't that the little black dog
with the yip-yip bark?

Chip!

What a smart dog! He didn't get lost at all.

51

Thanks for helping us catch Chip.

52

Kim, it looks as if you got your wish.

 Yes, Chip and I now have
some new friends in the city!

 Yip-yip! Yip-yip!

Think and Respond

1. Why do Kim and Dad rush out of their house?

2. How do Kim and Dad make new friends?

3. Do you think this story makes a good play? Why or why not?

4. Do you think Kim will like the city more from now on? Why?

5. Have you ever moved to a new place? Tell about your move.

Meet the Author
Wong Herbert Yee

At first Wong Herbert Yee only made pictures for children's books. Then he decided it would be interesting to write the stories, too.

"Did You See Chip?" is the first story Wong Herbert Yee has written as a play. He hopes that you will have fun acting it out in your class!

Meet the Illustrator
Laura Ovresat

Laura Ovresat loves to draw. She also loves dogs. She has a Labrador named Riley.

When Ms. Ovresat drew the pictures for "Did You See Chip?" she thought about the dog she had when she was little. That dog made her feel good, even when she was having a bad day. Does that sound like Chip?

Wong Herbert Gee   Laura Overrat

Making Connections

Farm or City?

Kim moves from a farm to a city. A farm and a city can both be nice places to live. What are some good things about each place?

Social Studies CONNECTION

Good Things

Farm	City
Animals	Tall Buildings

The Best Part

Writing CONNECTION

Which is your favorite part of the story? Draw and write about it.

I like the part when they found Chip.

New Friends

Math CONNECTION

How many new friends do Kim and Dad make? Who is the first one they meet? Who is the second? Who is the third?

1st 2nd 3rd

Setting

The **setting** of a story is the place where the story happens.

This is the setting for "Did You See Chip?" What is the setting? How can you tell?

Test Prep
Setting

 GEORGIA CRCT Tested Skill

Where Is Mark?

Mark feeds the hens and chicks. Next, he feeds the pigs in the pen. Then Mark feeds the animals in the big red barn.

What is the setting of this story?

○ a big city

○ a house on the shore

○ a farm

Tip

Read carefully. Think about the jobs Mark does to figure out where he is.

▲ Tomás Rivera

Word Power

Words to Remember

about

books

by

family

grew

read

work

writing

I **read** a lot of **books**. I have started **writing**, too. I want to tell **about** my **family**. I will tell how I **grew** up **by** a farm. **Writing** can be hard **work**, but it's fun.

Biography

A biography is a story that is written about a real person.

Look for:

- Information about the life of the person.

- Pictures that show what the person looks like and help explain what his or her life is like.

64

Tomás Rivera

by Jane Medina

illustrated by Ed Martinez

Tomás Rivera was born in Texas.
Tomás and his family went from
farm to farm picking crops.

Tomás helped pick crops all day. It was hard work. At night he had fun with his Grandpa.

"Come quick, children!" Grandpa
called. "It's time for stories!"

68

"You tell the best stories!" Tomás said. "I want to tell good stories, too."

"We can get lots of stories
for you, Tomás," said Grandpa.
"When?" asked Tomás.

70

"Let's go now!" Grandpa said
with a wink. "Quick, hop in!"

71

"This is a library," said Grandpa.
"Look at all the books!" yelled
Tomás as he clapped his hands.

"Read all you can, Tomás.
It will help you think of lots
of stories," said Grandpa.

Tomás read lots and lots of books.
He read about bugs, stars, and cars.

Tomás started thinking of
stories all by himself.

Tomás started telling his stories.
Then he started writing them.

When he grew up, Tomás got a job as a teacher. He still kept writing stories.

Tomás Rivera's stories tell about people picking crops, just as his family did.

Lots of people read his books.
They like his stories a lot.

Now his name is on a big library.
Many people visit the library.
They get books, just as Tomás did.

Think and Respond

1. What did Grandpa do at night for the children?

2. Why did Tomás want to tell his own stories?

3. How did Tomás learn to tell stories?

4. Why do you think Tomás Rivera wrote stories about people picking crops?

5. What kinds of books do you look for in the library?

Meet the Author

Jane Medina

Jane Medina teaches school in California. She read a lot about Tomás Rivera so that she could write this story about him.

Jane Medina hopes her story will help you think as Tomás Rivera did. If you work hard and do well in school, you can do anything you want to do!

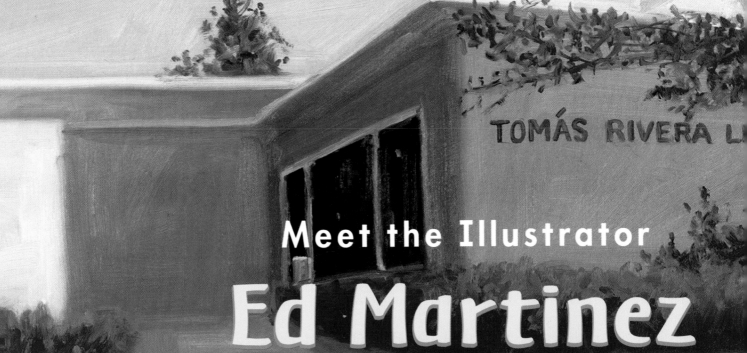

Meet the Illustrator
Ed Martinez

Edward Martinez used oil paints to paint the pictures for Tomás Rivera. He had to find out a lot of information before he started painting.

First, he found out that Mr. Rivera was born in 1935. Then he got photographs of people, trucks, and clothing from that time. He looked at the photographs as he painted. Do you think his pictures look real?

Edward Martinez

Making Connections

Helping Others

Tomás's Grandfather took him to the library. Tomás started reading lots of books. Think of a time that a family member, friend, or teacher did something nice for you. Tell about it.

Good Crops

What makes plants grow into good crops? Make a poster showing what plants need so they can grow.

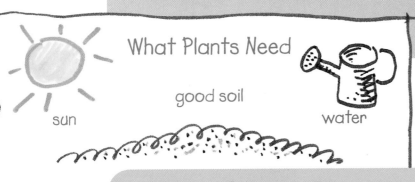

What Plants Need

sun

good soil

water

Your Own Family Story

Ask an older family member to tell you a story about someone in your family. Draw and write about that person. Share your story.

My great grandpa was a cowboy. He worked on a big ranch.

Characters

The **characters** in a story are the people or animals in that story. Here are some of the characters in "Tomás Rivera."

Who are the two most important characters in this story? How do you know?

student

Tomás

Grandpa

brother

Carmen loved to read. She liked animal books the best.

"What are you reading, Carmen?" asked Miss Quinn.

"It's a book about cats," said Carmen. "I like cats, a lot!"

"Me, too," said Miss Quinn.

CATS
by Candace Matthews

1. Who are the characters?
- ○ Miss Quinn
- ○ Carmen and Miss Quinn
- ○ cats

2. Who is the most important character?
- ○ Miss Quinn
- ○ Carmen
- ○ cats

Tip

Think about who is in the story. Who is speaking? Who is the story about?

▲ On the Way to
the Pond

Word Power

Words to Remember

find

follow

found

four

full

these

way

were

Tess and Herbert like to **find** new things. They saw **four** birds fly past.

"Where are **these** birds going?" asked Herbert.

"Come this **way**," said Tess. "Let's **follow** them."

They **found** **four** nests. The nests **were** **full** of baby birds!

Genre

Fantasy

A fantasy is a make-believe story.

Look for:

- Animals that talk.
- Animals that act like people.

On the Way to the Pond

written by Angela Shelf Medearis

illustrated by Lorinda Bryan Cauley

One day, Tess Tiger went to visit Herbert Hippo. They **were** hungry. Herbert packed a big basket for a picnic at the pond. It was **full** of good food.

"You bring the lunch," said Tess. "I'll
bring these four very important things."
Herbert looked at them and just nodded.

They started up the path. It was a very
hot day. All of a sudden, Herbert felt sick.

"Sit under my umbrella," said Tess.
"I'll fan you."

"Thanks," said Herbert.

When Herbert felt better, they went off to
the pond. All of a sudden Herbert stopped
and cried, "Oh, no! I forgot the basket!"

"I'll go back and get it," said Tess.
"You go on."

Tess dropped some rocks as she walked. She found the picnic basket and turned to go back.

On the way, Tess stopped. First
she looked this way. Then she
looked that way. She was lost!

"It's a good thing I dropped these rocks,"
she said. "I'll just follow them back."

Tess got to the pond, but she couldn't
find Herbert. "Oh, no! Herbert is lost!"
She got out her whistle. R-r-r-r!

"Here I am!" cried Herbert. "I'm glad you had all that important stuff!"

"Yes," said Tess, "and I'm glad you packed a big lunch! I'm starving!"

Think and Respond

1 What are Tess's four very important things?

2 Why are Tess's things important?

3 What problem do they have with the picnic basket?

4 How can you tell that Tess and Herbert are good friends?

5 How might the story be different if it happened in a snowy place?

Meet the Author

Angela Shelf Medearis

Angela Shelf Medearis loves to laugh and write silly stories. She has an office filled with toys. The toys give her ideas and make her laugh. She hopes that "On the Way to the Pond" puts a smile on your face.

Angela Shelf Medearis

Lorinda Bryan Cauley

Visit *The Learning Site!*
www.harcourtschool.com

Meet the Illustrator
Lorinda Bryan Cauley

It takes Lorinda Bryan Cauley about four days to draw the picture for one page of a book. First she does pencil drawings. Then she adds color with colored pencils and colored ink.

Lorinda Bryan Cauley works very hard on the characters' eyes. She thinks the eyes are very important for showing feelings. What do you think?

Hippopotamus

Hello, I'm a big happy hippo,
I sleep in the sun till I'm hot,
And when I'm not sleeping
I mooch in the mud,
Which hippos like doing a lot.

by Giles Andreae
illustrated by David Wojtowycz

Making Connections

After the Picnic

What can Tess and Herbert do after lunch? Draw and write your ideas. Share your work.

Writing CONNECTION

They can go for a swim.

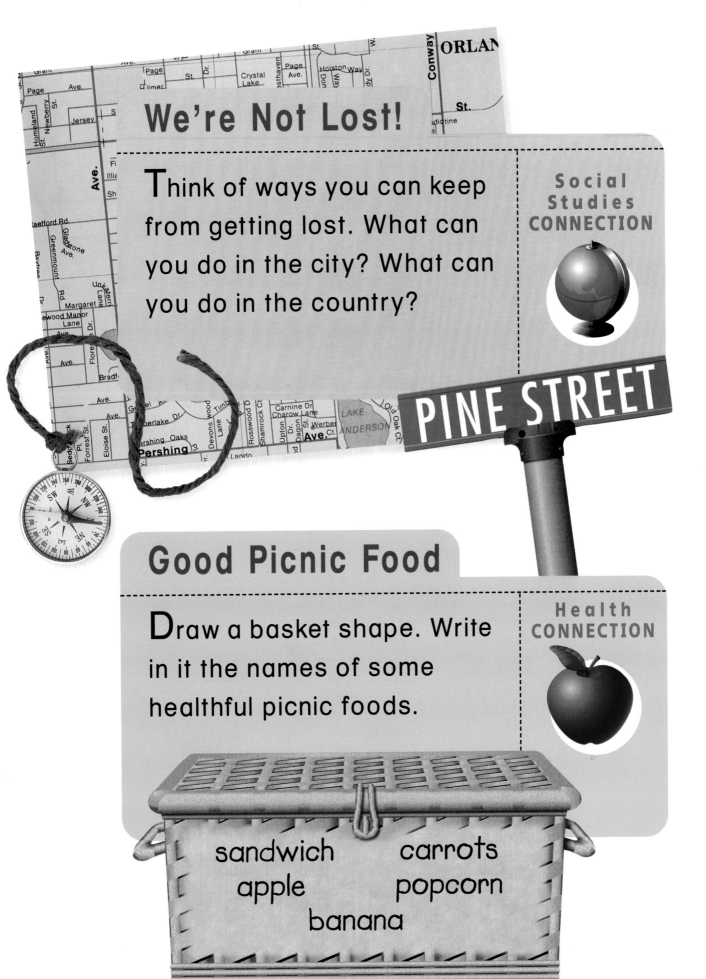

We're Not Lost!

Think of ways you can keep from getting lost. What can you do in the city? What can you do in the country?

Social Studies CONNECTION

Good Picnic Food

Draw a basket shape. Write in it the names of some healthful picnic foods.

Health CONNECTION

sandwich   carrots
apple   popcorn
banana

Setting

The **setting** of a story is the place where the story happens.

Which of these pictures shows the setting of "On the Way to the Pond"? How can you tell?

Where Are the Girls?

It's a hot day. Fish are jumping. The girls jump in, too. The cool water feels so good!

I. What is the setting of this story?

- ○ a desert
- ○ a lake
- ○ a food store

Tip

Read the story carefully and think about what the girls are doing. Then think about each answer choice.

Word Power

Words to
Remember

each

great

other

place

school

talk

together

112

Friends do things **together**.
Friends **talk** to **each other**.

What is a good **place** to
make friends? I think **school**
is a **great place** to make
friends.

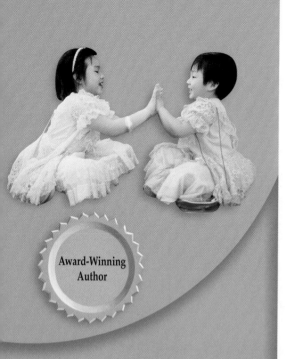

Genre

Nonfiction

Nonfiction describes books of information and fact.

Look for:

- Words that give information.
- Photographs that support the words.

Friends

Forever

by Ann Morris

We are good friends.

We play together.
We stick together.

We walk together and talk together.
We are glad to be together.

We help each other.

We can make a sad day a glad day.

We like to hunt for shells and rocks.
We dig.

Dig,
   dig,
      dig,

in the sand.

We have so much fun!
Let's jump up and down together.

Jump,
   jump,
      jump!

It's fun!

We eat snacks together.
We eat all sorts of food.

Munch,
   munch,
      munch!

Yum!

We whisper to each other and grin
and giggle.

Giggle,
   giggle,
      giggle!

Giggle with friends!

We're on a team.
We kick the ball.
We run and pass and kick and cheer.

Run,
run,
run!

Run with friends!

Sometimes we make bubbles.

Pop,
    pop,
        pop!

Sometimes we just like being together.

Let's make things—
red, purple, pink, or black.

Cut,
     cut,
          cut!

Let's act silly! This is fun!

We play a beautiful song together.

Fiddle,
fiddle,
fiddle!

Isn't that a nice thing to do with
a friend?

My granddad is my friend.
We catch fish.
We giggle when things are funny.
We hug a lot.

My little sister is my friend.

My dolls are my friends.

My horse is my pal.
My dog is my pal.

Pets can have friends.
My dog and cat are pals.

School is a good place for friends.
In school, we can share games and songs.

We can share books
and a smile.

Good friends are great!

Let's be **FRIENDS FOREVER!**

Think and Respond

1. Name some things that friends do together in this story.

2. Which activity looks like the most fun to you?

3. Besides people your own age, who else can be your friends?

4. Why is school a good place to make friends?

5. Do you think "Friends Forever" is a good title for this story? Explain.

Meet the Author
Ann Morris

Ann Morris always wanted to write a book about friends. "I love meeting people!" she says. "I like to travel and make friends all over the world. Friends are special no matter where they live. Good friends are always there when you need them." Here is Ann Morris with two of her good friends.

137

You'll Sing a Song

by Ella Jenkins

illustrated by Winky Adam

You'll sing a song, and I'll sing a song,
Then we'll sing a song together.
You'll sing a song, and I'll sing a song,
In warm or wintry weather.

and I'll Sing a Song

You'll play a tune, and I'll play a tune,
Then we'll play a tune together.
You'll play a tune, and I'll play a tune,
In warm or wintry weather.

Making Connections

Let's Write!

In "Friends Forever," some words are repeated just for fun. Make up a new page, using repeated words.

Let's make popcorn.

Crunch,

crunch,

crunch!

Share a Song

Work in a group. Practice a song you all like. Then perform your song for your classmates.

Music
CONNECTION

Shell Hunt

Find out some things about seashells. Draw a shell that you like. Show others where the animal once lived.

Science
CONNECTION

Words That End with le

The letters le can stand for the /əl/ sound as in apple. What is another word that ends with the /əl/ sound?

Name these pictures. Which picture does not have the le sound at the end?

Read these words from "Friends Forever." What sound do you hear at the end?

giggle	**bubble**
purple	**fiddle**

142

Test Prep
Words That End with _le_

1. **Which picture name has the ending sound for _le_?**

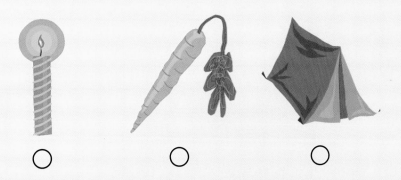

○   ○   ○

2. **Which picture name has the ending sound for _le_?**

○   ○   ○

Tip

Say each picture name slowly. Listen carefully to the ending sound.

143

Word Power

Words to Remember

door

kind

made

who

would

Fox looked out his **door**.
"**Who** **would** like to come in?"
he called. "I **made** popcorn
to share."
"How **kind** of you!" said
his friend.

145

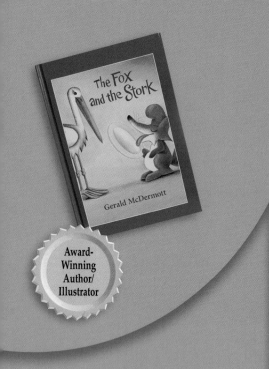

The Fox
and the Stork

Gerald McDermott

Genre

Fable

**A fable is a story
that teaches a lesson.**

Look for:

- **A lesson that you can
use in your own life.**

- **Animal characters
that talk.**

The FOX

and the Stork

retold and illustrated
by Gerald McDermott

Long ago there was a fox
who lived in the forest. Fox
liked to play tricks on
his friends.

One morning, Fox rowed his boat around the pond. He saw his friend Stork. "Would you like to come to my house for dinner?" Fox asked.

"How kind of you to ask!" said Stork. "Yes. I would like that."

The next day, Stork went to Fox's house for dinner. She tapped on Fox's door with her long bill.

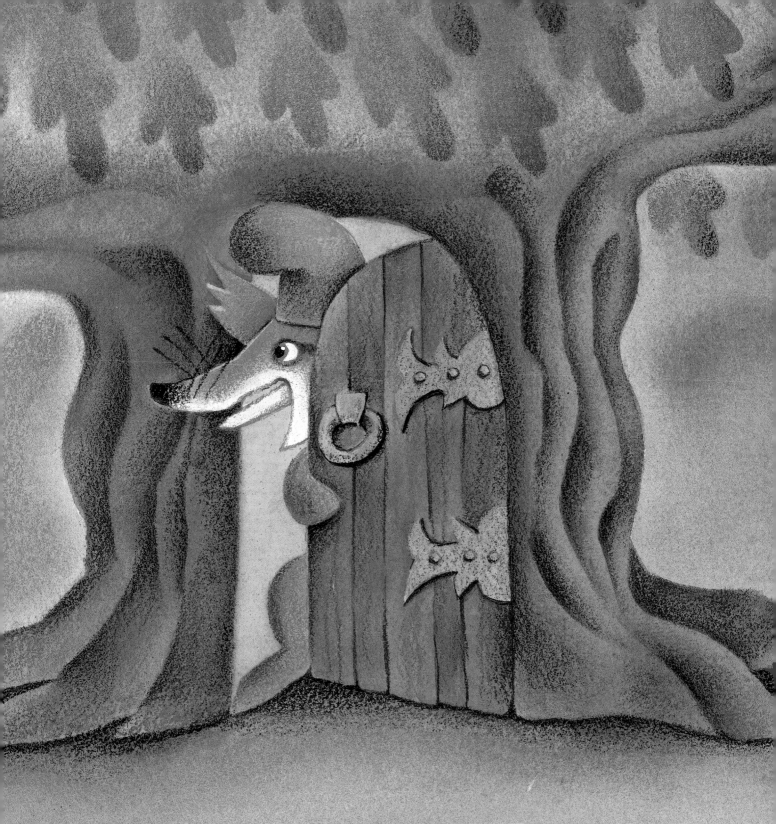

"Come in," said Fox. "I made soup!"

"Wonderful!" said Stork. "I like soup."

Fox and Stork sat down to eat.
Fox didn't put the soup in a bowl.
He served it in a flat dish.

Fox felt very smart. Stork couldn't eat
from the flat dish. All she could do
was dip the tip of her long bill into the
soup. Fox soon slurped it all up!

Stork was still hungry, but she didn't complain.

"Thank you for the dinner," said Stork. "Come to my house, and I'll make dinner for you."

The next day, Fox rowed his
boat to Stork's house.

"I don't like to boast," said Stork,
"but my soup is the best. I use
greens that grow in my own garden."

"Wonderful!" said Fox. "Let's eat!"

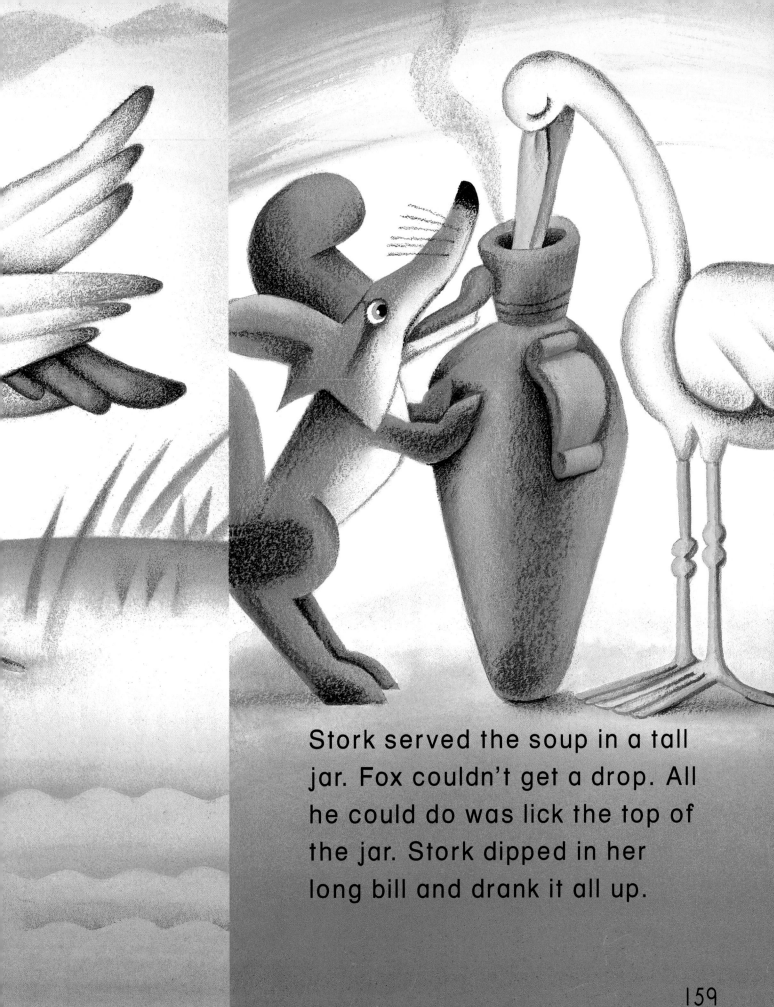

Stork served the soup in a tall
jar. Fox couldn't get a drop. All
he could do was lick the top of
the jar. Stork dipped in her
long bill and drank it all up.

159

Fox moaned and groaned as he rowed home.

"I'm so hungry! This is my reward for tricking a friend!"

At last Fox saw that being kind
to others is the right thing to do.

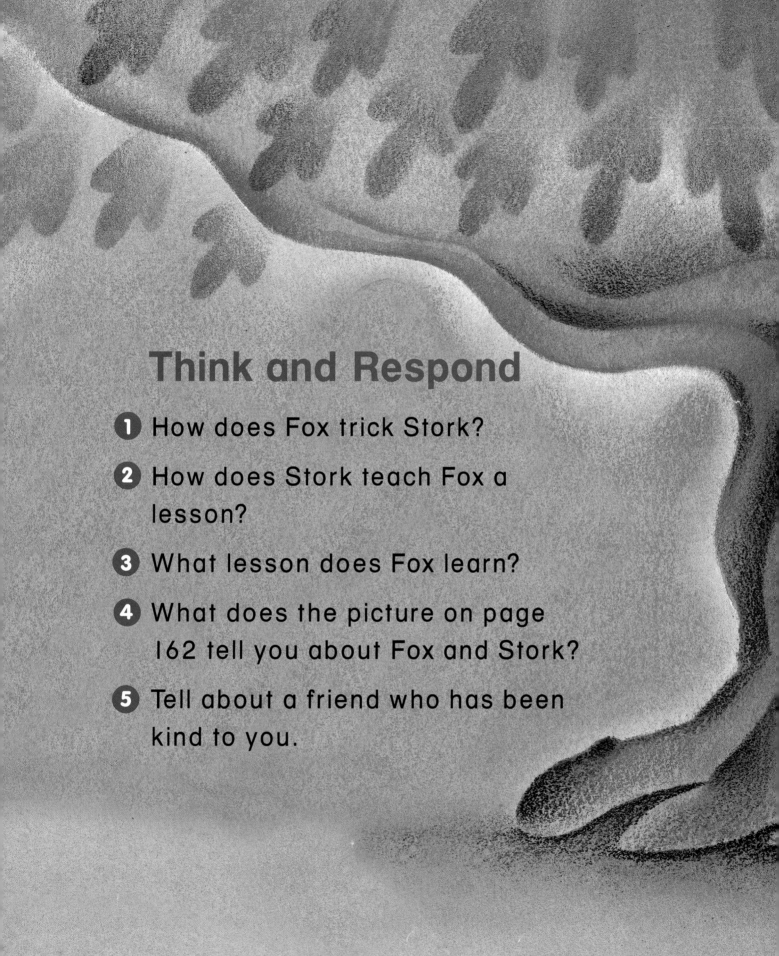

Think and Respond

1. How does Fox trick Stork?

2. How does Stork teach Fox a lesson?

3. What lesson does Fox learn?

4. What does the picture on page 162 tell you about Fox and Stork?

5. Tell about a friend who has been kind to you.

Meet the Author/Illustrator

Gerald McDermott

Visit *The Learning Site!*
www.harcourtschool.com

Gerald McDermott likes to retell fables and folktales because these stories have important messages. He uses his pictures to help tell the story and relate the message to his readers. Gerald McDermott hopes that you enjoy "The Fox and the Stork".

Foxes

by Barbara Parker

All foxes are dogs.
But not all foxes look alike.

Red Fox

The red fox has a white tip on its tail. It lives in the woods.

Arctic Fox

In winter, arctic foxes are white like snow. In summer, they are brown.

Gray Fox

The gray fox can climb trees like a cat. It hunts in the branches for birds and other animals to eat.

Bat-Eared Fox

The bat-eared fox can hear very well. It listens for termites and other insects to eat.

169

Making Connections

A Super Soup

Soup is a healthful food.
Make up a recipe for soup.
Put in all the good things
you like in soup!

Health
CONNECTION

A New Tale

Maybe Fox and Stork will be friends forever! Write about something they do together. Share your work.

Writing CONNECTION

More About Storks

Storks are interesting birds. Find out more about storks. Share what you learn.

Science/ Technology CONNECTION

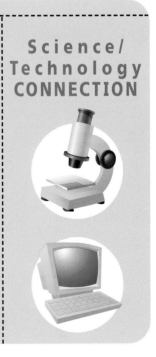

Characters

The **characters** in a story are the people or animals that the story is about. There are only two characters in the story you just read.
Who are they?

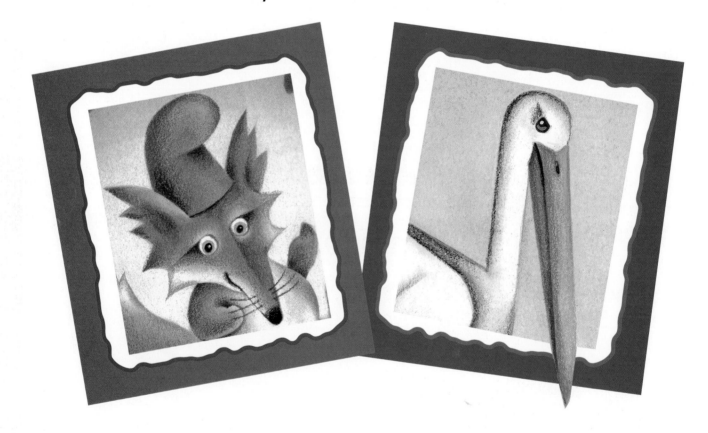

A Good Bird Friend

Crow was hungry. Sparrow had a lot of food.

"Come here, Crow," said Sparrow. "Come eat some of my corn."

1. **Who are the characters in this story?**
   - ○ Crow
   - ○ Crow and Stork
   - ○ Crow and Sparrow

Tip

Read the whole story before you answer. Read all the answer choices carefully.

Words for Writing

People Words

baby

boy

doctor

girl

mail carrier

man

police officer

teacher

woman

Names for Days

Sunday	Monday	Tuesday	Wednesday	Thursday	Friday	Saturday
		1	2	3	4	5
6	7	8	9	10	11	12
13	14	15	16	17	18	19
20	21	22	23	24	25	26
27	28	29	30	31		

Words for Writing

Names for Months

January

February

March

April

May

June

July

August

September

October

November

December

Things to Wear

belt

dress

hat

jacket

pants

shirt

shoes

skirt

socks

sweater

Glossary

What is a Glossary?

A glossary can help you read a word. You can look up the word and read it in a sentence. Some words have a picture to help you.

basket　　She has a **basket** of apples.

animals   Pigs are big **animals**. Ants are small **animals**.

basket   She has a **basket** of apples.

branch   The chipmunk stands on the **branch**.

cart   The man sells apples from his **cart**.

catch   I can **catch** a ball with one hand.

city   The **city** has a lot of people and cars.

drink   I like to **drink** milk with lunch.

180

farm   Cows, pigs, and hens live on a **farm**.

fiddle   Glenn can play the **fiddle**.

fly   A bird can **fly**. I can not.

giggle   That clown makes me **giggle**.

grin   A **grin** says that you are glad.

hatch   Soon the chick will **hatch** from its egg.

house   We live in a pink **house**.

nest   The **nest** has two bird's eggs.

park   The **park** has swings and a pond.

path   Quinn is walking on the garden **path**.

picnic   Ted and Janet have a **picnic** in the backyard.

read   I **read** books every day.

school   The **school** is made of bricks.

steps   Walk up the **steps**. Do not run.

under   The kitten hid **under** the deck.

web   What lives in that **web**?

wings   Bats have long **wings** to help them fly.

Acknowledgments

For permission to reprint copyrighted material, grateful acknowledgment is made to the following sources:

Ell-Bern Publishing Company (ASCAP): "You'll Sing a Song and I'll Sing a Song," lyrics and music by Ella Jenkins. Lyrics copyright © 1966, assigned 1968 to Ella Jenkins.

HarperCollins Publishers: "Mari Rosa and the Butterfly" from *The Tamarindo Puppy and Other Poems* by Charlotte Pomerantz. Text copyright © 1980 by Charlotte Pomerantz.

National Wildlife Federation: "Foxes" by Barbara Parker from *Your Big Backyard* Magazine, May 1999. Text copyright 1999 by the National Wildlife Federation.

Tiger Tales: "Hippopotamus" from *Rumble in the Jungle* by Giles Andreae, illustrated by David Wojtowycz. Text © 1996 by Giles Andreae; illustrations © 1996 by David Wojtowycz.

Photo Credits

Key: (t)=top; (b)=bottom; (c)=center; (l)=left; (r)=right
Page 8-9(all), Stephen Swinburne; 10(t), Stephen Dalton / Photo Researchers, Inc.; 10-11, 12, Stephen Swinburne; 13, E.R. Degginger / Bruce Coleman, Inc.; 14, 15, 16, Stephen Swinburne; 16(inset), 17, J&D Bartlett / Bruce Coleman, Inc.; 17(inset), 18, 19, Stephen Swinburne; 20, Kevin Byron / Bruce Coleman, Inc.; 21, John Gerlach / Animals Animals; 22, Stephen Swinburne; 23, L. West / Bruce Coleman, Inc.; 24, Stephen Swinburne; 25, Stephen Dalton / Photo Researchers, Inc.; 26, Dr. Eckart Pott / Bruce Coleman, Inc.; 27, 28-29, 28(t), 28(b), 29(l), Stephen Swinburne; 29(r), Rick Friedman / Black Star; 32(t), Stephen Swinburne; 32(c), Harcourt School Publishers; 32(b), 33(both), 34, Stephen Swinburne; 57(both), Santa Fabio / Black Star; 82, 83, 104(both), Black Star; 112(t), Superstock; 112(b), Ken Heyman / Woodfin Camp & Associates; 113, Bachmann / Photo Network; 114(l), Catherine Karnow / Woodfin Camp & Associates; 114-115, Superstock; 116, Catherine Karnow / Woodfin Camp & Associates; 117(l), Israel Talby / Woodfin Camp & Associates; 117(r), Bachmann / Photo Network; 118(l), A. Ramey / Woodfin Camp & Associates; 118(r), Ken Heyman / Woodfin Camp & Associates; 119, Michal Heron / Woodfin Camp & Associates; 120(l), G. Hofstetter / Photo Network; 120(r), Mike Yamashita / Woodfin Camp & Associates; 121, FPG International; 122, Esbin-Anderson / Photo Network; 123, VCG / FPG International; 124, Lori Adamski Peek / Stone; 125(t), Superstock; 125(b), Ken Heyman / Woodfin Camp & Associates; 126(t), Charles Gupton / The Stock Market; 126(b), Christina Thompson / Woodfin Camp & Associates; 127, Amy Lundstrom / Photo Network; 128, Catherine Karnow / Woodfin Camp & Associates; 129(t), Ken Heyman / Woodfin Camp & Associates; 129(b), Michael Keller / The Stock Market; 130, Arthur Tilley / FPG International; 130-131, Ken Heyman / Woodfin Camp & Associates; 131, Tim Davis / Stone; 132(t), Ariel Skelley / The Stock Market; 132(b), Nancy Sheehan / Photo Edit; 133, Harcourt School Publishers; 134(t), Bill Tucker / International Stock; 134(b), Camille Tokerud / Stone; 135, Catherine Karnow / Woodfin Camp & Associates; 136, McCarthy / The Stock Market; 137, Lisa Quinones / Black Star; 140, Superstock; 141, Harcourt School Publishers; 142(t), Superstock; 142(b), Ken Heyman / Woodfin Camp & Associates; 164, Black Star; 166-167, Daniel J. Cox / Natural Exposures; 166, Stephen J. Krasemann / Valan Photos; 168, Maslowski Wildlife Productions; 168-169, Theo Allofs; 178, 179(t), Amy Dunleavy; 179(b), 180, Superstock; 181, Ariel Skelley / Corbis Stock Market; 182(t), Tom & DeeAnn McCarthy / Corbis Stock Market; 182(b), Jose Luis Pelaez / Corbis Stock Market; 184(t), Ken Kinzie / Harcourt; 184(b), John Henley / Corbis Stock Market; 185(t), Julie Bruton / Photo Researchers, Inc.; 185, Roy Morsch / Corbis Stock Market.

Illustration Credits

Jerry LoFaro, Cover Art; Gary Taxali, 6-9; Amy Bates, 30-31; Steve Björkman, 32-33, 58, 85; Dona Turner, 34-35; Laura Ovresat, 36-57, 110; Jo Lynn Alcorn, 59; Liz Callen, 61; Ed Martinez, 62-84, 86; Taia Morley, 87, 173; Lorinda Bryan Cauley, 88-105; David Wojtowycz, 106-107; John Hovell, 109; Christine Mau, 110; Steve Haskamp, 111, 141; Winky Adam, 138-139; Stacy Peterson, 140-143; Gerald McDermott, 144-165, 171; Marina Thompson, 170-171.

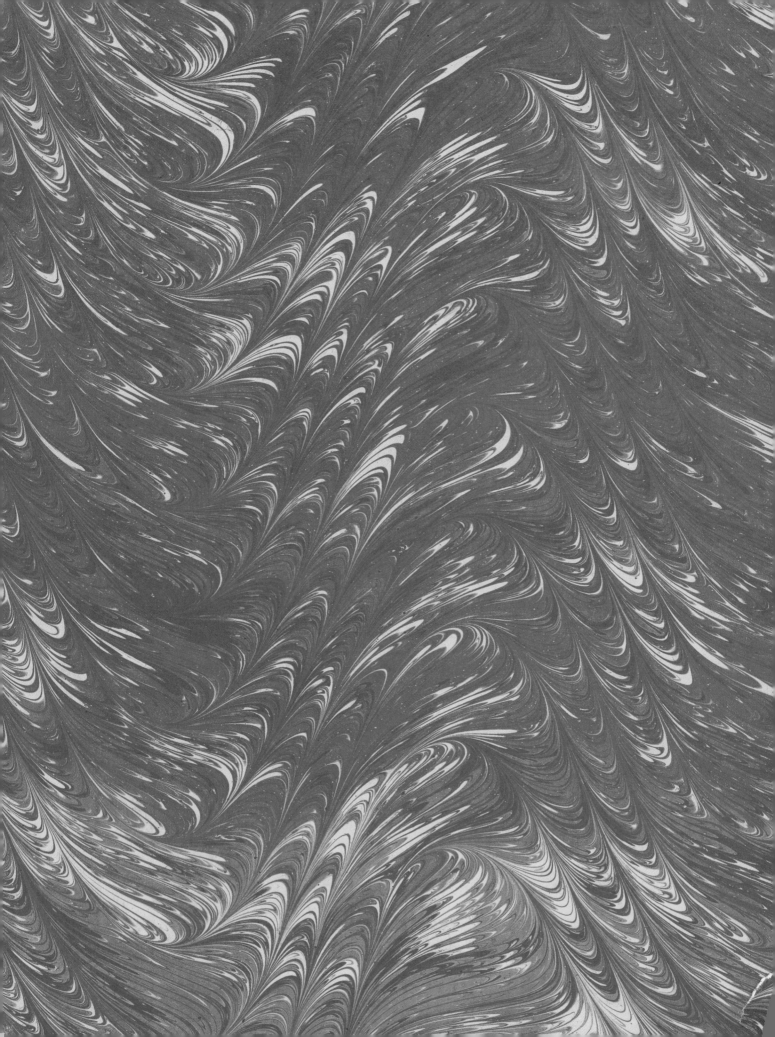